*This
path of
scattered
glass*

tom miller

This path of scattered glass

A collection of poems

Telcraft Books

in every poem
      there is Emotion
  and
in every Emotion
      there is poetry
          tm

Telcraft Books
3800 Mogadore Ind. Pky.
Mogadore, OH 44260

Copyright © 1993 tom miller
All rights reserved
Published by Telcraft Books in Mogadore, Ohio
Printed in the United States of America
10 9 8 7 6 5 4 3 2 1   3 4 5 6 7/9

Type set in 11 point Palatino on P.H. Glatfelter Co.
acid-free paper with more than 50% recycled fibers,
meeting the guidelines for permanence and
durability of the Committee on Production Guidelines
for Book Longevity of the Council on Library Resources.

May be reproduced for educational purposes in the
buying teacher's classroom, but not for resale. Write
publisher for permission for reproduction for other use.
∞
Publisher's – Cataloging in Publication
(*Prepared by Quality Books Inc.*)

miller, tom, 1961–
   This path of scattered glass: a collection of poems /
tom miller.
   p. cm.
   ISBN 1-878893-39-4 (pbk.)

   I. Title.

PS3563.I865.T45 1993   811'.54
                                        92-84067
                                        QBI93-8

For Ms. Sturkey

dear respected teacher
    from my past
i have, too, grown older
    and bolder
      but, have not moved
        towards the rewards
of all my time and effort

have i sown NOTHING
    to reap?
have i nothing to keep
save a clutch
    of thensandwhens?
or am i blind to all that i find
  on this path of scattered glass?

        tom
        8/29/84

"to feel a poem"

to read a poem

with your eyes

you must not read

with your eyes

you must not see

with your eyes

you must live

with your heart

and you must feel

with your soul

contents

foreword *forward*—what are you feeling . . . ?   *13*
about the author   17
todays and tomorrows   18
Hey, Lord, remember me . . . ?   21
will it fall?   22
the poetry is there   24
Rosewood—the rose in the woods   25
AREN'T I DANCIN' MUCH TOO FAST!?   28
i fumble with my own words   29
semi-conscious and unaware of the Air   30
CERTAIN PEOPLE   32
CRYSTAL BLOOD BROTHERS   35
PARANOIA   36
COLD_____TRUTH   38
BEFORE THE MOVE   40
the vee in the tree—a story   43
self-(dis)repair   53
self-repair   54
"FROZE"WOOD   55
diamonds   59
another leaf of life   60
my sweet sister moon   61
Weighty Words   64
i shall sit in a wood   66
i hear movement upstairs   67

(continued)

waxing words   69
tapestry   72
THIS GENERATION   73
LIPS ALLOWED   74
so many times i've written   75
THE OUTPOURING   76
Literary self-doubt and reassurance   77
fear or terror or mirror   78
the miscarriage   79
onion skins   80
THIS IS STILL-LIFE   81
contents of my dead sister's wallet   83
Second thoughts of a poet   86
in hopes that you might re-invent words   87
sowing, singing and searching   88
Comment on ATLANTIS   90
ATLANTIS   91
only if and when   92
the leap of life . . .   94
AFTERWORD *onward*   96

foreword *forward*

what are you
       feeling at this
              moment?

why did you
       pick up this book?

Those feelings alone are a poem.

I've grown up watching people cringe and shy away from poetry. Watching as people, cannot or choose not to accept or get/grasp poetry.

Poetry is simply words that we write. When we write a letter to a friend, *that* is a poem. Even when we write a grocery list—
       or hang our laundry

that is a poem . . .

washday

aren't we simply
       clothespins
upon a white and vinyl line

    trying to
      make
      some
      sense
      of
      the
      dirty
      laundry
      to
      which
      we
      cling?

tm
7/24/83

If you write words upon a page about anything . . . and an image, a picture is roused in the mind of a person who is reading your words, then you have succeeded.

Writing, to me, has *always* meant making *those* pictures in others' minds. Panoramas, situations, emotions for which i have fought to find—and the words therein all to define.

I can't be sure that i would be able to find those words now, had i not been shown the electricity that others have felt as i actually wrote my heart, my words, upon pages—for them to find, to see, and to read—feeding—recognizing a part of each themselves.

                      write your words down
                        before you
                          forget
                                them . . .
           don't be so cruel as to let them
                                    stray

                              away—from
                          a joy or a pain

           away from another
                 who is joyous or pained

      let—
            your joy—
                    your pain
                          become something
                    attained
                          and shared

                            by another
                        sisterbrotherother

The most important thing about writing is that you are always writing about yourself.

No matter the matter or the character(s), each bit that you write is a bit about you . . . for you to save, to hold to read again and again.

I can tell you truthfully, that if you keep a "diary of your thoughts"

>—for a long time
> for—
> > a long time

> that diary of thoughts

> > will tell you things

> > > that you had long forgotten
> > > about your Self . . .

For the memories that I am able to retain because of each of my poems

> i want to thank the people
> *who* are my *poems*

Whether or not they recognize themselves in pieces of my work, they are there. Each and every one of my family and my friends, at one time or another, become either a phrase in or the backbone of a poem.

I am grateful to live around such a myriad of poempeople.

> i hope that each of you
> enjoy my poempeople, too

> and enjoy the peoplepoems
> that surround each and every

> > one of you . . .

> > > tm
> > > 11/1/92

about the author

i was young, when i met poetry.

i was born, just outside of akron, ohio, september 27th, 1961—at 2:15pm.   at 2:16pm, i met poetry—screaming—poetry.

life is poetry.

i was young, when i met my own words. i was in-troduced to them in september of 1973, by my seventh grade "language arts" teacher.

Ms. Sturkey encouraged me to find my own words.   more importantly, she helped *me*, a shy person, to write my words upon a page, for others to read.

if you read a few of those words—those words— my poetry—will tell you far more about me . . .

than i usually tell about

my
    Self . . .

tm
12/10/92

todays and tomorrows

each day begins
        just as the day before
as i wipe
        sleep from blurred eyes
smoking—drinking myself
        awake

        i have no plans
            of cures for cancer
or means of feeding
            poverty-stricken
              masses
only hopes
    that i shall
      pass this day
without pangs of boredom
    that plague me
        locking me
          in a chair
          in my room

bound in throes of thought
    of all that could be done
      —i know that i
        shall visit none
of my great castles
    in the air
    —today

    but—
bound in throes of poetry
        and prose
    have i raised
        a pen—a purpose

            to fill again
                        another leaf or two
            all for myself
                        all for you
            in hopes that all
                        i do

                        all i write
            might show an ink-ling
                        of Truth and insight

                        as the words
                        eternally flow
                        from thought
                                    to arm
                                    to hand
            to page

                        i work with symbol
                                    and image
                        striving to find
                                    from behind
                                    blind eyes

                        the questions
                                    i ask
                        for are the answers
                                    about
                                                —within me
                        if only knew i
                                    what i seek

        this morning
          as i
            swig another
        swallow of life

              dancing onward into
                the night
              when i shall
                bury myself
              in my typewriter
              in my love

              in hopes that

tomorrow . . .

                            tm

Hey, Lord, remember me . . . ?

Hey, Lord, remember me
                      —the one who prayed for a dream

Well, Lord, i need ya' now—well again i mean

Can ya' give me a hint—about where i'm to go

           Or at least could ya' give me a little rest?

I ask for but a word or two

           a spark—a wink—a whisper

Just give me a star and a nudge from behind

           an exit from the labyrinth
For the riddle perplexes far beyond compare
'Cause i'm tired of

                        circles&cycles&worn out dreams
And thought of perpetual pursuit

           of the fantastical pot of gold
                  and fear of the road not taken

For the forest's too dim
        the trees too dense

        And i'm lost in the morning mist

Ya' see, Lord   i'm scared

        and i just want a little hug

                to help me find my way . . .

                                tm

will it fall

this mighty house
    does creak
      and sway
   in whipping winds
       about
 but a thought
     a dream
  a prayer
might keep the tiles
    from blowing
     from the roof

  can it stand
      will it stand
    another heave
     upon its eaves
  relentless squalls
      upon its walls

     i see a whirling wind
    in perilous pressing approach
      notwithstanding
       my demanding
     threatening to encroach

 with no where to hide
   no place inside
to cower away the hours
    of fear forever
     lurking 'bout here

  damn the waif
     no longer safe
    in time sanctified
       space

a base
 a place
    away
       from this

 no longer safe,
       poor orphaned waif
    living lies
          incessant cries
              for
                        Love
          and safe
              safe
                 ties
       of family and friends

can i stand
         will i stand
    another squall
             upon my wall
    or will it fall
             to shattered pieces
          neatly 'bout my
                       feet

          will it fall
                will it fall
       and will
             i stand
          above
              throughout
       without
                      it
                     all?

                            tm
                         11/22/82

the poetry is there

the poetry is there
            within each of us
      it lies inside
            our hearts and souls
   existing in the trails of our tears

          yet—
             lost as it seems
         behind our facades
         and our games

the poetry is there—
      in our tenderest thoughts

and in our most violent rage

it hides in our every move
    fighting to survive
        the coolness
           of the absence
              of our touch

and try as we might
    to ferret it fast
    to the finest holes
    of our tattered hearts—

still it lives on—

        for if the poetry
        is there no longer

no longer are we . . .

                tm
                4/2/80
          revised 10/21/92

Rosewood—the rose in the woods

There must be a pressure
                                  felt in a rose bud
              bud of a flower—before that flower
                            EXPLODES
                      into beauteous   *GLORIOUS*
                      star-colored life
and musn't that — pressure — *AUGMENT GREATLY!!!*
                            a volcanic quake
                    or earthquake's
                        tremorous shakes

        forewarning   foreboding
there must be   a pressure
        felt in a flower's bud
   at the moment before it explodes
     a once held
once smelled
     scent
       spent
                      before its time

          THERE MUST BE AN IMMENSE PRESSURE
              felt in a bud before it blooms . . .
  and i
      KNOW
        that—   i *feel*   it now
  as impending as a climax
      that cannot be slowed   controlled
          or *MAN*ipulated

as rough as a course   —   uncalculated
         a voyage unmapped
         a tourist slapped
               in a
          fragrant, foreign world
i finally feel the desire to live
            again—further   farther
              than i've ever lived
god forbid
     that i will be as wreckless as i've been—
               unmapped and virtually
                 —unslapped
               by the reality
                 of all that
                     is
                       about
                       within   me
                       and those
that live— about— within—
                          me . . .

HELP TO SLAP SEE ME BACK INTO THE BLACK AND WHITE
         REALITY—
                          that it be
              the pressures felt
         in a bed of
             similarly
               colored
                 shaped   and soiled
                soul flowers

                        abouttobleed   and bloom
                            while sitting alone
                                again with one
                    —and another
                                        as — each —
                                            we see

            hungers for a rebirth
                    that still remains in silent strains
                        of pain and quiet crying

                                    from fear of succeeding
                                            or bleeding
                                    the guilt and pain   out of

                                        each our own

                                        wicked, tired

                                                        selves

        each of us

                            SITTINGSLEEPING WEEPING

                                    keeping

                                        warm
                                        upon
                                        these
                                        spaces
                                        we've
                                        allotted
                                            to
                                        our
                                        SELVES!

                        UPON THE PERPETUALLY LEADEN
                                                    laden

shelf—that each we've made from ROSEWOOD!
                                        tm
                                        1/04/88

AREN'T I DANCIN' MUCH TOO FAST!?

aren't i dancin'
                        much too fast!?
                for the beat of the song
                  should move me slowly
                    —a leaf awaft
                        upon the wind

    instead—am i not
                      atwitch ajerk
              verging berserk

            chasing my tail
                    careening an arc
                    afraid that i'm stark
                        raving
                  mad

    i have rolled the past
        a time at a time
  all in a ball
      beneath
    me

        and yet i fear
            i cannot appear
            to stay aroll
                atop
                a balled-up knot
                of nowandthens
                and whens

forlatelastnightthismorning
        did not i chase a rat
                forever fat and black

      until it turned
              and chased me back?

                        tm
                      2/14/82
               revised 10/4/92

i fumble with my own words

    i fumble with my own words
                yet—i know that i am making perfect sense
and you smile and nod
                        as if comprehending
        all that i say

yet—   you don't understand   you can't understand

        all of the pain which i have absorbed
and even as you look upon the lines of my verse
    i wonder that perhaps   a few tears
                an iota of the hurt
    might filter through the fog

                and softly touch the core of your
                        emotions
nonetheless—   you are polite   as you sit and listen

    and i can truly say that i appreciate that
    for not everyone would do such a kindness to me

                &
perhaps one day   your eyes will open to the words
        that you have heard in the past
and you will remember the pain that another has felt

        and maybe the memory will ease
                a bit of the pain you feel . . .

                            tm
                          2/7/80

semi-conscious and
   unaware of the Air . . .

elementarily—
    all about
is of Air and Earth
is of Water
  and
  Fire
raw-blazing in the hearts
  of candles
     of Us

and we burn of our selves
   of Change

  fed on
   all about
  of Air and Earth
  and of Water

     consumed
     by the
     Tides
      by the
       Moon
swept in strains
    of Avatar
  down and
    around
   and then again
  upward
    and then again
around
  all about
  of all directions
  of all ways
    and for ever

         yet — we
          walk about
           our lives
    of Earth and Air
    of Fire and Water
            —elementarily
              Us

       unaware
        that we are
         who we are
    of the Stuff of the God
    of Earth — of Water
        of Fire
         within us

  semi-conscious and unaware
            of the Air —

                    tm
                 5/27/82

CERTAIN PEOPLE

i am simply
        the sort of person

    that *certain* sort of person

      who loves certain people

and enjoys having

        certain people
      around me

          alot . . .

      certainly not

           strange
           of me

but— certainly a strange part of me
        is having a certain

       problem

      about finding that

            certain person . . .
     to full
        fill
             me

      unlike the
           rest of my

                 certain people
        canwillareallowed

            to
            by

            me

         and certainly only

                   as
                   i

                    allow

certain things to get
                  by
                  me
     i only allow
certain things to get
                into
                me . . .

          i am selective
              must be certain

                 that there'll be not
                      hurtin'

                    not again

34 / This path of scattered glass

                                                                       certain
                                                                         not to be

                                                        hurtin'

                                                                             and holdin'

another certain person

        uncertain

             that
               they
                 are

    the one . . .

                                           tm
                                     1/10/88

CRYSTAL BLOOD BROTHERS

AND THE CRYSTAL
    SLIPPED FROM MY FINGERS
    SLIPPED FROM MY GRASP
    SLOWLY SLIPPED
        AWAY

he asked me to take his knife
    to cut him
    to cut myself
    to be blood brothers
        i was afraid

AND THE CRYSTAL
    SPED TO BE SHARDS
    SPED TO BE SHATTERED
    SPED TO BE LED
        AWAY

i wanted to take his knife
    to open him
    to open myself
    to be soul brothers
        of this i am not afraid

THE CRYSTAL
    SLIPPED and shattered
    MY heart
    and SLIVERS
    and shivers
      ABOUNDED
    and i was astounded

        that both
        he and i
        bled

        tm
        7/2/87

PARANOIA

in the piranha filled waters of your
paranoid mind

i lurk
in stealth
and stay
i make my way
from within your blackest fears

most wicked tears
to churn
to burn
your heart

and as you dream
i shall scream

black narrations
the sick fascinations
than truly are
YOUR OWN

and as you sow
so shall you weep
so watch yourself
as you do sleep

     as there i stalk
    as there i creep
   to haunt
   to taunt
  to stunt
   only you
    for i
    for i
    am
     only you
   trying
   to undo
   you . . .

all by yourself

     tm
    8/15/87

COLD _____ TRUTH

i see your evil
    and
      raise you

    one
    cold-blooded
      TRUTH

      in this game of life
      that you and i play

        you seem
          always
        to have
         something
        to say

and i —
    for the most part
    am cold-loved
      silent

but, nevermore
    there sayeth
      my Self
    for i am tired
      of you
      screaming ME

        down
        a clown in
          YOUR EYES

when — with my eyes
i've overlooked
your crooked
wily
ways —

— let you believe
that you've
gotten away
with something

when —
actually —
factually

you've
deceived not
anyBODY

but your own

and that's
a —
my —

COLD _____ TRUTH . . .

tm
12/8/87

BEFORE THE MOVE

to love myself
        i love another

  a wife
    a mother
     beloved blood brother
  in causing pain
       i find no gain
    simply put
      it's a game
        insane

    so i've set myself
    by loving those around me

    dear God — surround me
    with those who'll
      love me back

        tm
       7/28/87

a story

THE VEE IN THE TREE

"Shall I forever continue to be
A fanciful boy on a branch in a tree
Never willing to venture the vee,
Never daring to climb past me?"

    The last remnants of a late August rain dripped cooly from the leaves of the yellow cherry tree. Jared stood beneath its expanse, gazing upward into the tangle of shiny, wet limbs. Occasionally, he would spy a drop from high above, moments before it splashed, a startle, upon his upturned nose. Playing tag with raindrops, however, didn't hold his seven-year-old interest for very long. For every child knows that a *yellow* cherry is good for only one thing—climbing to the sweetest cherries, forever at the top.

Jared firmly grasped the lowest limb of the familiar tree and hoisted himself routinely upon it. He sat holding the branch above his head. Letting his warm, blond hair pull outward toward the ground, he leaned back further, languidly looking long into the light through the limbs. He pondered the highest twigs of the tree and the thrill of throwing his eyes out over the yards upon yards that he could see in his mind, but not with his eyes—something he'd never seen before.

As he lazed upon the lowest limb, a rush of certainty sped through him, as if icy waters had washed over his heart. With eyes intently locked upward, he knew in himself that today was not for play. *It* was there—before him—above him—just for him. He wanted so much to be able to climb higher than he ever had before—to climb past the vee in the tree, over which he had always been too tiny to triumph.

He resolutely began to climb his usual pattern up the moist, deep-red branches, watching as the fork in the thick trunk loomed ever closer above him.

In the distance, he heard someone faintly calling his name.

"Hey! Wha'cher doin', Jary?" the voice cried again, coming closer to the tree.

Jared looked down through the limbs to see who was there.

"Hey yourself, Adam," he called down from above, as his young friend ducked under the tree. "What's it look like I'm doin'?"

Adam's muddy, freckled face squinted into the sunlight which silhouetted Jary in the myriad of limbs and leaves. He brushed his sopping, red hair from his eyes and visored his hand. "D'ya wanna go over to the mud hill? Everybody's over there! We're havin' a mud war and they told me I could play if I could get you to be my partner."

"Not right now—I'm climbing. Why don't ya' wait for me?" Jared said as he pulled himself up higher, ignoring his friend's insistence.

"Come on, Jary! They all sent me over to get ya'. You can climb this dumb ol' tree anytime."

Jared undauntedly continued to scale the slippery limbs, until he stood with his feet solidly wedged in the fork of the tree. He looked down at Adam, who was dancing impatiently at the foot of the tree, occasionally kicking its weathered trunk as he looked up at his friend.

"Come on down now, Jary. You can't climb any higher."

Jared shook his head and smiled. He looked up as he had done so often and contemplated the next limb. It was so far out of reach above his head. If only, he thought, there was just one little stub of a branch in the vee, then he could step up a little more.

He looked back down at Adam. Maybe he was right—he could climb this tree anytime—everyone was waiting for him—besides, he couldn't climb any higher anyway. As he shifted his weight from his tightly wedged foot, preparing to climb down, a most startling revelation grabbed him . . . if he were to securely plant his foot on the side of the fork beneath the next limb, then, perhaps he might be able to quickly push upward and grab the base of the branch above. Without thinking of the consequences of failure, he rushed upward and in one fluid movement was hanging from the branch, his feet dangling above the vee.

"Jary!" Adam gasped. "What are you doing!?"

"What's it look like I'm doin', stupid!? HELP me!"

"Let's go, Jary! Come on—CLIMB DOWN!"

Jared struggled to get his feet onto the trunk beneath the branch. His thin arms quivered as his sneakers spasmodically slid from the wet wood. A fearful cry began to form in his throat. The terror of impending failure rushed upward into his face as did the ground when he looked down.

Calling upon every young sinew of strength in his panic-stricken frame, he determinedly pulled himself up, until he was able to swing his leg over the slippery branch to which he was climbing. Panic pounding in his temples, he locked himself safely to the strong wooden arm.

Adam pranced nervously about the base of the tree. "Come on, Jary—" he insisted, "before you fall!"

"NO WAY!" Jared breathlessly exclaimed as he pulled himself up to stand cautiously upon the limb. "I'm climbing up to the top!"

"You're crazy—come on. Let's go!"

Adam's persistence only pushed Jared higher into the thinner branches near the top of the tree. The wind had dried most of the rain from the highest twigs at the top, making the climb go faster and more sure-footed.

Jared marvelled at the ever-shrinking trunk and at the ever-widening view that broke through the thick of limbs and leaves. He felt like one of the black crows that always dined in the very top of the tree, freely eating cherries and squawking toward the earth below. On the last of the limbs large enough to support him, he stood, holding fast to the tapered shaft of the tree-trunk, as it swayed in the wind. His blue eyes crinkled in satisfied smile as he lingered aloft, lordishly looking over the land below. The vee was far beneath him now. His mind scarcely considered getting back down. Clinging high above it all in liberation, he knew that he had made it.

He craned his neck around until he could see the mud hill, far behind him. A few of the boys, bouncing around in the mud, appeared to be facing in the direction of the tree. Jared could barely see them, though. He wanted to wave to them, but he didn't dare let go of the limb. Gusts of wind blew the treetop around every now and again, whipping the branch to which he was fastened.

"What's it like up there?" Adam shouted to the sky. "Are the cherries sweet? What can you see? Would you help me up there? Hey, Jary—throw me down some cherries!"

Jared laughed to himself as he noticed how few cherries dangled about him. As he cautiously reached out to pluck a bunch which hung behind him, another gust of summer wind shook him on the branch, so high above his friend. The limb swept earthward, bending down until the trunk cracked noisily. Jared tensed against the tree, hoping that the limb would not snap under his weight.

"Help *me* climb up there, Jary!" Adam insisted as he started up the first branch of the tree.

"No—I'm coming down," Jared muttered as he carefully found good footing to start his downward climb. "Let's go over to the mudhill, now. I want to tell the guys about climbing to the top!"

"But *I* want to climb to the top, too!" Adam demanded as he climbed into the vee in the tree.

"Go ahead—but, I'm getting down and I'm not gonna help you up. You'll have to do it yourself—like me."

"Come on, Jary!" Adam pleaded.

Jared solidly refused to help as he climbed down upon the branch above the gap. He told Adam to move out of the fork so that he could get down. Still wanting very much to climb higher, Adam reluctantly climbed down from the vee in the tree.

Jared waivered on the branch, contemplating the ever-widening gap beneath him. It looked so much wider from above. He carefully maneuvered himself closer to the trunk. He hoped that he could swing down next to the tree, then simply slide down the trunk to the vee.

He firmly grasped the branch and dropped his legs into the gap. His feet scraped coarsely into the trunk, his body swinging erratically in the vee. He struggled and kicked at the trunk, finally clamping it tightly between his legs. He dangled from the limb, momentarily, attempting to regain his courage and breath.

He could feel his fingers slowly slipping from around the wet, red branch. Beneath him, he could hear Adam's incessant babble hurrying him. He was happy that no one could see him hanging there like a fool, scared to let go. He knew that he either had to let go, or he was going to fall anyway. He wondered why he had ever wanted to climb so high in the first place. If he fell, he would probably break his neck, and if he wasn't hurt, his friend's laughter would surely break his heart.

His grip failing, he let go of the branch and clung desperately to the trunk of the vee. His chin scraped fiercely over its bumpy, red bark as he slid to a sudden stop. His stomach tightened in excruciating pressure and his breath stopped painfully short. Vee to vee, he straddled the tree, bloody-chinned and nauseous.

"Are you coming or not, Jary?" Adam again insisted.

Jared struggled to free himself from the grip of the fork. He managed to get his foot onto the next branch and shakily floundered out, noting his scraped and bloodied chin. He had *really* made it, he realized. The blood on his chin proved it.

He wanted to hurry home to his mother's concern and care, but getting to the guys at the mud hill was much more important. Maybe one of them had even seen him so high up there. In any case, Adam would vouch for him. *He* was here. He will tell them how Jared had been—how fearless and successful and high and big he had been in making it past the gap to the very top of the cherry tree.

"Come on, Jary. I think it's startin' to rain again," Adam urged, trampling in the mud beneath the tree.

"Okay already! I'm comin'!" Jared retorted as he

hurried down the familiar branches beneath the vee. He was happy that he had decided to climb higher than he ever had before. He couldn't wait to tell his friends.

"Look out! I'm coming down," he warned Adam. "Get out of the way!"

Jared hastened onto the last branch. In his rush, his foot slipped from the wet, muddy branch. He felt his stomach tense as he plummeted backwards. In a glorious splash and grunting thud, he landed flat upon his back, knocking the wind from him.

Again bound in the folds of muddy earth at the base of the tree, he lay, dazed and dismayed. The treetop swayed high and free above his motionless body, as drops from the top splashed tauntingly upon his upturned nose.

> "Shall I forever continue to be
> A fanciful boy on a branch in a tree,
> Never willing to venture the vee,
> Never daring to climb past me?"

tm

poetry

self-(dis)repair

i've been banging my face
    into the mirror
    of my mind

  in a vain attempt
    at changing

  my self-image

    and — once again —
    i draw back
    sore and disappointed
    realizing

that i've blackened both of my eyes
  and broken my own nose
    to spite my own face

  cut my self down
    to make myself taller

torn my own hair out
    because i've gotten balder

  made myself
    worse off

    than i was
    before i
    started
    trying
    to
    change

  myself . . .

        tm
        12/19/87

self-repair

        today
  i

    took

       the mirror

       from my bathroom . . .

                tm
              12/19/87

"FROZE"WOOD

an arctic breeze
    blows
        strong and fast
            through these
                solemn
                soulful
                southern
                states

recounting rhymes
    of other times
  renaming names
    and
      thoughts
        sublime
            a wet and frozen
              winter chime
            of another thought
              from another time
      frozen as —
        i was a child
  frozen as a rose arisen
        in the forest of
            myself
      each new experience
           each new
              query
              hence
        has held
            and spelled
      in crystal shards
          knotted yards of
          the yarn
          of
          yarns

the absence of the
                    goal
            the gold
                    of the whole
        a silent, cold
                and golden
                    mole
                        frozen
                            in a frigid
                            blindness
                                of rigid
            molded   molding   roles
        a dead and dying
                frightful scheme
                    the end of all that's
                        seemed to've been
    the salvation of myself
            a snap
                in a link
                    of a bound
                        and
                            bittered
                        hand-cuffed
                                hell

            a personal slam

                    a self-destroying
                        magical spell

            afrozenfrigidrigidstifflieabout
                            my
                                    cold
                                and
                            frigid
                    frozen

                                    self . . .

a warmth within
           seeming a sin

   a good
        and gathered
                giving thought

                that perhaps
                         i ought
        to   give myself
                    a
                break of belief
                        and relief
           and trust that all is well
                with my self
           and in my life about as well

begin to melt the
           personal Hells

  to clean up the
           dirty feet
                smells
                    about
                    and
                    around
                    my
                life and self

        at least to
            sweep
      this dusty

            self-made
                rosewood
                    shelf

upon which i've

        chosen
     to tarry to wait

     frozenfrigid

                      tm
                     1/88

diamonds

can you really know

                        a person

      in all that you see
           of a person
                in a life

     andyouseethemeverydayeveryway

     all that you are seeing

  a r e s c a t t e r i n g . . .

                      reflections
                          of a distant
                             fire

a star burning below the horizon

                      you see the light
              dancing behind the eyes

     but you never

          stand before the blaze

              of the God

                    within

so you must
close your eyes
and see them

      through the eyes
         of the One in you . . .

              tm
           9/8/80

another leaf of life

night surrounds my sleepless bed
                        a dim, unanswered question

    and fear and fear — it dances near
                        seducing with suggestion

the woven worms of weary thought
                        wind again upon themselves

        twisting and entwining
   tightly writhing in the rut of worry and of fury
      a brooding brook of judge and jury

        for i seem to pass my days along
        a failing echo of a distant song

        and i again approach anew
        with querulous strains of what to do
        an age — a page — and passage to
                      another leaf of life.

                                  tm
                              1/1/84

my sweet sister moon

. i'm erupting —
      a raging
     NUCLEAR hell!

    either take her all
      or leave her whole
     but always protect
         her innocent soul
      a sweet and blessed
       sister moon

why is this happening?
  is it to show me
    that I can
    take this
without needing to be
     carried

two sets of footprints
      instead of One
is *that* why *this* is being done!?

has she led
    her life
so well
  so good
    done everything
      that she knew
       she should

    that
my sweet sister moon
  should die so soon
her life wrapped up
  a gift to God
her body interred
    again to the sod

her face returned
    again to the sky
for me to watch

  at night to cry
    WHY!!?
because —
    it's the time and
      the space
in which it should happen

as perfect as a flake of
      snow
foretelling winter's frigid blow
and battles retold blow for blow

  as i walk in black
    through absent snow
    beneath the glow
of my sweet sister moon
  who leaves my side
    all too soon

i'll always love you sister mine
my sweet and blessed sister moon

    FOR DEANNA MILLER
    6/20/63 – 10/26/87

TO MY FAMILY —

    in dying —
        Dee is fulfilling
            herself

        her death
          has made us a
            family again

        drawn each of us
          closer to one another

    and that's
        a special thing —

        worth dying *for*

          tm
        10/26/87

Weighty Words

perhaps i have waited too long
                  hung too long   too high in the clouds

        i've watched the world below with
                              envy
yet—deep in the mire
           i half-struggle   to free myself

    while multitudes stand about
                drawing attention to my struggle
                    and still   they offer me not
their aid—a simple gesture
           which might lift me from
                  my ever-apparent fate

and still   all they give
                are words   emotionless words
    while i am sinking deeper
        with the weight
      of all of the empty words

perhaps—if i lie very still
      they will think me dead
                  and pull me out
   but, i have been eternally still
      and they slowly move away

                              unmoved

and even i   have moved from myself

                                            in escape

    yet, i am still bound to the me in the mire

               no longer am i visible
to anyone   even me

      i am again secure
                   in my surrogate womb
          hidden from the pain of the words

it's very hard to distinguish   though

   between a womb

             a cocoon

   and a grave

                             tm
                            1/21/80

i shall sit in a wood

i shall sit in a wood
      a slight clearing
      with a white and wooden seat
            just for me

animals shall come to me in the wood
      delicate creatures
      shall comfort and calm me

i shall sit in a wood
      surrounded by fragrance
      by flowers and buds of multiform color
            just for me

love shall come to me in the wood
      from all and none abounding
      within without with calm

i shall sit in a wood
            shall you sit with me?

tm

i hear movement upstairs

      i hear movement upstairs

and i hope that i've awakened   no one

          to awaken anyone as i taptaptap
    here in the basement

                alone

again i sit   smokefromasmolderingcigarette

    f i l l i n g   t h e   r o o m

  hoping to find a   few words of wisdom

    to fill this page

these are the times when i huddle close within myself

                reaching inward   pensively

pressing buttons and watching my thoughts emerge before me
      like soldiers aligning for inspection

  and perhaps a neighboring soul will hear the tap
          or smell the smoke of another of my thoughts
as it finds its way from my heart to the paper

    but he will move onward   undaunted by the tiny

   noises and smells which rise from beneath

and perhaps he will even fret   momentarily

     hoping that he has not disturbed . . .

                        i hear movement downstairs

and i hope that i've disturbed no one

           to disturb anyone   as i shuffle to the fridge

   alone in the kitchen

again i search

           for a few bits of nourishment
             to fill my restless stomach

these are the times when i huddle close within myself

                        reaching inward   pensively

   quietly digesting my food and thoughts

and perhaps a neighboring soul will hear the shuffle of my slippers
           or the click of the refrigerator door
as i prepare for another personal tête à tête with myself

         but he will move onward undaunted by the muffled

      clatter of another hungry insomniac
           searching for midnight snacks and quiet thoughts

and perhaps he will even fret   momentarily

          hoping that he has not disturbed . . .

      i hear movement upstairs

                            tm
                         9/26/79

waxing words

as i slept
        i crept
                into the closet of my heart

    awakening to find
               within my mind

                my soul—
            and my heart—
          a gold mine—
                 of my own!?

*   *   *

worried, furrowed, frail lines
           all about myself
       stood ready at "ATTENTION"
         each word aligned
                 upon its shelf

   and carefully have i each night
        held each these soldiers near

     waxing words

             upon a page

         hoping . . .
                                you will . . .

*   *   *

     here, i have found
            the words like
                   waters

                   floating lilypads about

no more the old gnome grinding grist

        in the hidden dale of
                his

                      Self

                           who
                           whirls
                           his worlds
                           like

                                  waters

            floating sillythoughts about
              about
                  helping others
                  when i barely
                    help
                         my Self!?

     just who
          does this
               elf on a shelf

            hidden deep

                 within

                      himself

        think he is!?

   *   *   *

here, have i found
    my own words

                      lurking

          around . . .

      to be found
                    only when i needed
            to see them . . .

and carefully have i each night
      held these soldiers near

           waxing words
                upon a page

        hoping . . .

                you will . . .

    sleep and creep
        into a closet of your heart . . .

                      tm
                  10/18/92

tapestry

i tacked
a rug—
a tapestry
on

my wall all to
applaud
to stand
and

to gaze
at for all time
my forever
facade

tm
1981

THIS GENERATION

This generation . . .
        what will we be?
Something the world
        has been waiting to see?
It's been beat through our heads
        that we have to be great!
And now that is something
        we're beginning to hate.
There will be doctors and
        lawyers and teachers galore,
But others want something
        a little bit more.
We want to be us
        just simple and true.
Not that that was planned
        and built and drew.
We want our own life
        and our own direction.
Not something that's simply
        this society's reflection.
Not plastic, machines,
        life ending at thirty,
We want to live long
        and get our hands dirty.
Be happy, spontaneous,
        loving, alive
Not having to fight
        in this world to survive.
So, let us be us,
        and you can be you.
No cramping, no binding,
        just honest and true.
This generation . . . ?
        let's see what we've got.
Then we will see if
        we'll make it or not.

tm

LIPS ALLOWED

i have watched those lips
   so firm and fleshy
      for hours upon days
   have hung on those lips
      for words they've formed
         but always
saved

words of love
   words of trust
      words of tender
         burning lust

and once or twice
   as you've allowed

i've lingered on those lips so proud

to taste your sweet and sacred song
   though you never allowed
   that i linger long

          tm
         5/7/88

---

so many times i've written

a verse

—words

then suddenly seen them

       tm
      5/80

THE OUTPOURING

you cannot force a tear
    or it shall lose its reason
and i have been awaiting
    the coming of the cry
for so very, very long

    in the quiet of the eve
i've felt its pulse within
and i've wanted it to be
    terribly

if, but, one drop of sadness
    could
    find its way
       from my heart
         to my eye . . .

    tm
    6/20/80

Literary self-doubt and reassurance

what's happening!?

where are you!?

        lost words
            old friends
                and loves

        are you hiding!
            from me?

oh—you've been here on this page

        all along . . .

tm
1/14/88

fear or terror or mirror?

i seem to have lost

my identity

self worth
and sanity

what a futile calamity

should i return
the mirror

to my bathroom?

tm
2\3\88

the miscarriage

it's been said that you can't miss

    something you've never had

how cruel
   that there *is* an exception
      to every rule
for a child has been lost
   at such a caustic cost

a child never held
   or loved as it would have been

   had it won its struggle
     into this harsh
       and harried world

a flicker of love
    extinguished
   leaving two hearts
    in anguish

who said that you can't miss . . .

          tm
         6/3/88

onion skins

        old man   wise man
sitting in your chair

      why do you peel onions
of their layers—sitting there?

you watch with fascination
        as brittle and brown skins
    do crackle and give way to
       their tender white withins

    and yet you peel onward
            crying with a sigh

searching truth in onion skins

            who and why am i?

      tm
    12/2/84

THIS IS STILL-LIFE

moss has gathered
                                 upon my pond
        the spot where i retire

                when things confuse
                and goals diffuse

                it's been a place of safe refuge
                away from the mucking mire

    but–what of the moss
        what *is* the cause

                of this scum upon my thoughts

            is it overlooked wishes—
                        and shoulds and —

                            oughts

                surfacing now
                    after
                all these years
              —rotting mold upon
                  rotting beers—

pervading my mind
>> perverting my pond

>> is this the legacy
>>>> i will spawn!?

or will i drink and think—
>> and then smoke and choke
> until i remember when

>> my pond was clear
>>> and i could hear

> my quiet times alone
>> when moss was merely something

>>>> that never gathered on a rolling

>>>>> stone.

>>>>>> tm 5/30/91

contents of my dead sister's wallet

                                    i never went to my sister's
                                                funeral
                                  it was not that i didn't love
                                                  her . . .

    *   *   *

there are often
        deep
            secrets
                hidden
                    amongst
                        siblings
                samesiblingsecrets

                        that we are either
                            too—ashamed
                                  or
                            too—scared
                                    to share
                            with any other
                                    than . . .
       samesiblingssecretsamesouls

    *   *   *

i returned to my
        sister-less home
        a decided pause . . .
        after the fact—
                —that she had died
        to find the fact
                that i have not cried

                        about her actually
                              having passed
                                    heavenlyskyward

                        for—to me—
                                that is not something to be
                                            mourned—
                                        but—embraced
            and yet—my mother
                    wanted each my brothers
                        and me
                            to have
                                a piece
                                a peace
                                    of Dee—
                                -my sweetsistermoon-
        and—she gave me
                the wallet that
                    my sister died owning—

                        her *wallet*

                                pictures
                                money
                                words
                                and whys
                                        intact
and a driver's license that would have expired, if . . .

*   *   *

                        if—i had not seen
                                the contents of my
                                dead sister's wallet—

i would not have known

            that she died with a condom
            in her wallet
            for protection . . .

or that she died with but a dollar bill
                and some change
        that was all to her name—
                      in her wallet—

to save her childson
    her adorationcreation

all of the pictures—
    photos of friends . . .
        and "stay as you are and you'll go far" . . .

*   *   *

i wish i had had
    better protection
        from the contents
            of my dead sister's wallet . . .

for, it bites at my heart—
a carnivorous creature

    eating a hole in
    the whole in me . . .

    eating at the
    samesiblingsecrets
    that are eating at

        me . . .

                tm
                11/5/92

Second thoughts of a poet
(Shall i release my pen?)

Shall i release my pen
And cast it to the current
To squelch the flow of words and lo—
To search my rut and then to pace
My self-made, muted grave

And should i care that in the air
A flash of wayward wisdom—
A word, a truth or ounce of hurt
A simple syllable—
Might sing a heaving heart to sleep
Or ease an aching, silent weep

To dam the stream of ink and life
Filling barren leaves of white
To snuff the flame of candle-hours
Succumbing to the night
Shall i release my pen
And turn my back unto the Light?

*   *   *

Take my breath—or take my life
Bleed me—cut me with a knife!
For like moths to flames am i to words
Lit by Fires—lighting lines
Dancing diametric dreams
Of all that is and all that seems
For my last hours may fill pages
Talking Time or singing sages

Shall i forever clutch my pen
    And all my thoughts in blue
  Casting words upon the waves
    Reaching out
                     to you . . .

                      tm

in hopes that you might re-invent words

in hopes that you might re-invent words . . .

       re-invent

                re-discover!

   one another

       and an
           other
              may

            dis-

           re-

          un-
                cover

                      you . . .

                            tm
                        10/18/92

sowing, singing and searching

as i meander
    the Garden of my Mind
dodging the
    budding twigs
of seedlings therein

my heart senses
    my nose tenses
at the scents
    of Death
    about
        me

and i notice
    that no one
tills the moist
    springearth
no more
    the old gardener
sitting on the side
    of his sweet soil bed
sipping beer
    like wine
        —admiring

    no more
        the oldgardener
laid now
    to sleep
        drunken
            in the folds of
    sweetsoils
and silent
satisfaction

                    knowing
               that the young man
          who cries ink
               upon pages
           and counsels with
                    sages
     is coming
                         of age
          the tiller

               no more
                 the old gardener
            but the
                    boy
           who sits smoking songs
       of his
                    self
                on the side
                of his
                    sweetsoilbed

         admiring —
                    meandering
               ink upon leaves
          and seeds into souls

                         and soils
                    sweat fed and
                         tenderly
                    furrowing
                ever deeper
                    ever longer
                    for
               ever
     sowing singing and
                    searching

                         tm
                    4/20/81

Ms. Turkeyn

This is an "original" copy of a poem that i wrote when i was in the hospital when i had overdosed on tranquilizers, purposefully, when i was sixteen.

You helped to teach me, without knowing, that it's better to bleed upon a page,

than to bleed upon a floor...

Jm 9/23/92

ATLANTIS

be it not a caged dove
nor a flightless eagle
but a baby bird without a nest
in search of a Mother
in search of a Father
in search of a Love
only to flee   to be
i am a fish
drowning in the river of Chagrin
i am an infant
from the security of the womb
of a barren heart
be it now that i must be
the maternal breast
the paternal strength
yet am i not   my love
a stranger   a benign soul
seeking a shelter
from my dreams
to return to a scarred womb
of an age of old   only to find cold
in the place of a once raging flame
only a spark — only dream
only a broken hourglass

tm

only if and when

if only i had touched your face
    as you — touched
        my heart
but —
  PEOPLE
  just aren't
    allowed
  to do that
      that which
      HASMIGHTCAN
      change a heart
      make it start . . .

if only i had touched your face
  as you have touched my heart

    *   *   *

i have walked
  a long, hard way had a lot to say
  about everything every day
    and i've written it
      down

i'm touching you . . .
    now . . .
  in the only way
    that i know how
i'm reaching out
    to touch your face
  with the words that
    form
  upon this page

    age . . .

if only
    if only
WHEN ONLY only when
    i really reach out
        to touch —
            your face

will your words grace
    and cradle me

a soft and subtle sweet embrace
        to brace me
        for

        more . . .

                tm
            9/18/92

the leap of life . . .

```
let us be not
            mining
       minding
                  minds

            let us be
                   expanding
       the
            minding minds of the rhymers
            of each their times
            as each they are
                        there
```

for plastering one's heart
      upon a page

is a bungee jumpleap
a slice of self seeped
      upon a page

for us to keep
      either
      for ourselves

      or
      for
      others

sisters and brothers

      who make

the leap of life.

      tm
      10/19/92

shall forever
continue to be...

AFTERWORD *onward*

born was i—

                        unto a path
                        of strewn
                            and shattered
                                  glass

      a path which led me
         a path which bled me

        a path
            that slashed

            then patched me

              up

                    for more
and i've learned that

though Life and Strife may seem to rhyme

                they *are* not one
                and the same

for one does tame
            while the other claims

        bloodied
        shoeless

                    victims.

                    tm
                12/31/92